A/75/49 (Vol. II)

Resolutions and Decisions
adopted by the General Assembly
during its seventy-fifth session

Volume II

Decisions

15 September – 31 December 2020

General Assembly
Official Records • Seventy-fifth Session
Supplement No. 49

United Nations • New York, 2021

NOTE

The resolutions and decisions of the General Assembly are identified as follows:

Regular sessions

Until the thirtieth regular session, the resolutions of the General Assembly were identified by an arabic numeral followed by a roman numeral in parentheses indicating the session (for example: resolution 3363 (XXX)). When several resolutions were adopted under the same number, each of them was identified by a capital letter placed between the two numerals (for example: resolution 3367 A (XXX), resolutions 3411 A and B (XXX), resolutions 3419 A to D (XXX)). The decisions were not numbered.

Since the thirty-first session, as part of the new system adopted for symbols of General Assembly documents, resolutions and decisions have been identified by an arabic numeral, indicating the session, followed by an oblique stroke and another arabic numeral (for example: resolution 31/1, decision 31/301). When several resolutions or decisions were adopted under the same number, each of them has been identified by a capital letter placed after the two numerals (for example: resolution 31/16 A, resolutions 31/6 A and B, decisions 31/406 A to E).

Special sessions

Until the seventh special session, the resolutions of the General Assembly were identified by an arabic numeral followed, in parentheses, by the letter "S" and a roman numeral indicating the session (for example: resolution 3362 (S-VII)). The decisions were not numbered.

Since the eighth special session, resolutions and decisions have been identified by the letter "S" and an arabic numeral indicating the session, followed by an oblique stroke and another arabic numeral (for example: resolution S-8/1, decision S-8/11).

Emergency special sessions

Until the fifth emergency special session, the resolutions of the General Assembly were identified by an arabic numeral followed, in parentheses, by the letters "ES" and a roman numeral indicating the session (for example: resolution 2252 (ES-V)). The decisions were not numbered.

Since the sixth emergency special session, resolutions and decisions have been identified by the letters "ES" and an arabic numeral indicating the session, followed by an oblique stroke and another arabic numeral (for example: resolution ES-6/1, decision ES-6/11).

In each of the series described above, the numbering follows the order of adoption.

*

* *

The present volume contains the decisions adopted by the General Assembly from 15 September to 31 December 2020. Resolutions adopted by the Assembly during that period appear in volume I, together with information on the allocation of agenda items. Resolutions and decisions adopted subsequently during the seventy-fifth session will be published in volume III.

ISSN 0252-7014

Contents

Decisions

Page

A. Elections and appointments 4

B. Other decisions 10

   1. Decisions adopted without reference to a Main Committee 10

   2. Decisions adopted on the reports of the First Committee 20

   3. Decisions adopted on the reports of the Special Political and Decolonization Committee
      (Fourth Committee) 23

   4. Decisions adopted on the reports of the Second Committee 24

   5. Decisions adopted on the reports of the Third Committee 27

   6. Decisions adopted on the reports of the Fifth Committee 29

   7. Decisions adopted on the reports of the Sixth Committee 30

Annex

Checklist of decisions 33

Decisions

Contents

Decision number	Title	Page

A. Elections and appointments

75/401. Appointment of the members of the Credentials Committee 4

75/402. Election of members of the Human Rights Council 4

75/403. Election of members of the International Court of Justice 4

75/404. Appointment of members of the Advisory Committee on Administrative and Budgetary Questions 5

75/405. Appointment of members of the Committee on Contributions 5

75/406. Confirmation of the appointment of members of the Investments Committee 6

75/407. Appointment of members of the International Civil Service Commission 6

75/408. Appointment of members of the Independent Audit Advisory Committee 7

75/409. Appointment of members and alternate members of the United Nations Staff Pension Committee 7

75/410. Election of members of the Committee for Programme and Coordination 7

75/411. Election of the United Nations High Commissioner for Refugees 8

75/412. Appointment of members of the Committee on Conferences 8

75/413. Election of members of the Organizational Committee of the Peacebuilding Commission 8

B. Other decisions

1. *Decisions adopted without reference to a Main Committee*

75/501. Organization of the seventy-fifth session 10

75/502. General debate of the seventy-fifth session of the General Assembly 10

75/503. High-level meeting to commemorate the seventy-fifth anniversary of the United Nations 10

75/504. Adoption of the agenda and allocation of agenda items 11

75/505. High-level meeting of the General Assembly to commemorate the seventy-fifth anniversary of the United Nations 11

75/506. Introduction of certain reports in the plenary meetings at the seventy-fifth session of the General Assembly 12

75/507. Report of the International Residual Mechanism for Criminal Tribunals 12

75/508. Report of the International Court of Justice 12

75/509. Report of the Economic and Social Council 12

75/510. Procedure for decision-making in the General Assembly when an in-person meeting is not possible 12

75/511. United Nations Pledging Conference for Development Activities 14

75/542. Investigation into the conditions and circumstances resulting in the tragic death of Dag Hammarskjöld and of the members of the party accompanying him 15

75/554. Agenda items remaining for consideration by the General Assembly at its seventy-fifth session 15

Decision number	Title	Page

2. *Decisions adopted on the reports of the First Committee*

75/512. Reduction of military budgets ... 20

75/513. **Maintenance of international security – good-neighbourliness, stability and development in South-Eastern Europe** ... 21

75/514. Further practical measures for the prevention of an arms race in outer space ... 21

75/515. Treaty banning the production of fissile material for nuclear weapons or other nuclear explosive devices ... 21

75/516. Nuclear disarmament verification ... 21

75/517. Compliance with non-proliferation, arms limitation and disarmament agreements and commitments ... 21

75/518. Missiles ... 22

75/519. Disarmament Commission ... 22

75/520. Provisional programme of work and timetable of the First Committee for 2021 ... 22

75/521. Programme planning (First Committee) ... 22

75/550. Open-ended Working Group on Developments in the Field of Information and Telecommunications in the Context of International Security established pursuant to General Assembly resolution 73/27 of 5 December 2018 ... 22

75/551. Group of Governmental Experts on Advancing Responsible State Behaviour in Cyberspace in the Context of International Security established pursuant to General Assembly resolution 73/266 of 22 December 2018 ... 23

75/552. Problems arising from the accumulation of conventional ammunition stockpiles in surplus ... 23

3. *Decisions adopted on the reports of the Special Political and Decolonization Committee (Fourth Committee)*

75/522. Comprehensive review of the whole question of peacekeeping operations in all their aspects ... 23

75/523. Question of Gibraltar ... 24

75/524. Proposed programme of work and timetable of the Special Political and Decolonization Committee (Fourth Committee) for the seventy-sixth session of the General Assembly ... 24

75/525. Programme planning (Special Political and Decolonization Committee (Fourth Committee)) ... 24

4. *Decisions adopted on the reports of the Second Committee*

75/543. Macroeconomic policy questions ... 24

75/544. Globalization and interdependence ... 24

75/545. Groups of countries in special situations ... 25

75/546. Operational activities for development ... 25

75/547. Draft programme of work of the Second Committee for the seventy-sixth session of the General Assembly ... 25

75/548. Revitalization of the work of the Second Committee ... 27

75/549. Programme planning (Second Committee) ... 27

Decision number	*Title*	*Page*

5. *Decisions adopted on the reports of the Third Committee*

75/537.	Promotion and protection of human rights	27
75/538.	Comprehensive implementation of and follow-up to the Vienna Declaration and Programme of Action	27
75/539.	Countering the use of information and communications technologies for criminal purposes	27
75/540.	Draft programme of work of the Third Committee for the seventy-sixth session of the General Assembly	27
75/541.	Programme planning (Third Committee)	29

6. *Decisions adopted on the reports of the Fifth Committee*

75/553.	Questions deferred for future consideration	29

7. *Decisions adopted on the reports of the Sixth Committee*

75/526.	Protection of persons in the event of disasters	30
75/527.	Provisional programme of work of the Sixth Committee for the seventy-sixth session of the General Assembly	30
75/528.	Programme planning (Sixth Committee)	31
75/529.	Observer status for the Cooperation Council of Turkic-speaking States in the General Assembly	31
75/530.	Observer status for the Eurasian Economic Union in the General Assembly	31
75/531.	Observer status for the Community of Democracies in the General Assembly	31
75/532.	Observer status for the Ramsar Convention on Wetlands Secretariat in the General Assembly	31
75/533.	Observer status for the Global Environment Facility in the General Assembly	32
75/534.	Observer status for the International Organization of Employers in the General Assembly	32
75/535.	Observer status for the International Trade Union Confederation in the General Assembly	32
75/536.	Observer status for the Boao Forum for Asia in the General Assembly	32

A.   Elections and appointments

75/401.   Appointment of the members of the Credentials Committee

At its 1st plenary meeting, on 15 September 2020, the General Assembly, in accordance with rule 28 of its rules of procedure, appointed a Credentials Committee for its seventy-fifth session consisting of the following Member States: CAMEROON, CHINA, ICELAND, PAPUA NEW GUINEA, RUSSIAN FEDERATION, TRINIDAD AND TOBAGO, UNITED REPUBLIC OF TANZANIA, UNITED STATES OF AMERICA and URUGUAY.

75/402.   Election of members of the Human Rights Council

At its 16th plenary meeting, on 13 October 2020, the General Assembly, pursuant to its resolutions 60/251 of 15 March 2006 and 65/281 of 17 June 2011, elected BOLIVIA (PLURINATIONAL STATE OF), CHINA, CÔTE D'IVOIRE, CUBA, FRANCE, GABON, MALAWI, MEXICO, NEPAL, PAKISTAN, the RUSSIAN FEDERATION, SENEGAL, UKRAINE, the UNITED KINGDOM OF GREAT BRITAIN AND NORTHERN IRELAND and UZBEKISTAN as members of the Human Rights Council for a three-year term of office beginning on 1 January 2021 to fill the vacancies occurring on the expiration of the terms of office of AFGHANISTAN, ANGOLA, AUSTRALIA, CHILE, the DEMOCRATIC REPUBLIC OF THE CONGO, MEXICO, NEPAL, NIGERIA, PAKISTAN, PERU, QATAR, SENEGAL, SLOVAKIA, SPAIN and UKRAINE.

As a result, as of 1 January 2021, the Human Rights Council is composed of the following 47 Member States:[1] ARGENTINA,* ARMENIA,** AUSTRIA,* BAHAMAS,* BAHRAIN,* BANGLADESH,* BOLIVIA (PLURINATIONAL STATE OF),*** BRAZIL,** BULGARIA,* BURKINA FASO,* CAMEROON,* CHINA,*** CÔTE D'IVOIRE,*** CUBA,*** CZECHIA,* DENMARK,* ERITREA,* FIJI,* FRANCE,*** GABON,*** GERMANY,** INDIA,* INDONESIA,** ITALY,* JAPAN,** LIBYA,** MALAWI,*** MARSHALL ISLANDS,** MAURITANIA,** MEXICO,*** NAMIBIA,** NEPAL,*** NETHERLANDS,** PAKISTAN,*** PHILIPPINES,* POLAND,** REPUBLIC OF KOREA,** RUSSIAN FEDERATION,*** SENEGAL,*** SOMALIA,* SUDAN,** TOGO,* UKRAINE,*** UNITED KINGDOM OF GREAT BRITAIN AND NORTHERN IRELAND,*** URUGUAY,* UZBEKISTAN*** and VENEZUELA (BOLIVARIAN REPUBLIC OF).**

---

*   Term of office expires on 31 December 2021.

**   Term of office expires on 31 December 2022.

***   Term of office expires on 31 December 2023.

75/403.   Election of members of the International Court of Justice

The General Assembly, at its 24th plenary meeting, on 11 and 12 November 2020, and the Security Council, at its 8773rd meeting, on the same dates, proceeded independently of one another to elect, in accordance with Articles 2 to 4, 7 to 12 and 14 and 15 of the Statute of the International Court of Justice, rules 150 and 151 of the rules of procedure of the Assembly and rules 40 and 61 of the provisional rules of procedure of the Council, five members of the Court for a nine-year term of office beginning on 6 February 2021 to fill the vacancies occurring on the expiration of the terms of office of Mr. Giorgio Gaja (Italy), Mr. Iwasawa Yuji (Japan), Ms. Julia Sebutinde (Uganda), Mr. Peter Tomka (Slovakia) and Ms. Xue Hanqin (China).

Having obtained the required absolute majority of votes in both the General Assembly and the Security Council, Mr. Iwasawa Yuji (Japan), Mr. Georg Nolte (Germany), Ms. Julia Sebutinde (Uganda), Mr. Peter Tomka (Slovakia) and Ms. Xue Hanqin (China) were elected as members of the Court for a nine-year term of office beginning on 6 February 2021.

As a result, as of 6 February 2021, the International Court of Justice is composed as follows: Mr. Ronny ABRAHAM (*France*),** Mr. Mohamed BENNOUNA (*Morocco*),* Mr. Dalveer BHANDARI (*India*),** Mr. Antônio Augusto CANÇADO TRINDADE (*Brazil*),** Mr. James Richard CRAWFORD (*Australia*),* Ms. Joan E. DONOGHUE (*United States of America*),* Mr. Kirill GEVORGIAN (*Russian Federation*),* Mr. IWASAWA Yuji (*Japan*),*** Mr. Georg NOLTE (*Germany*),*** Mr. Patrick Lipton ROBINSON (*Jamaica*),* Mr. Nawaf SALAM (*Lebanon*),** Ms. Julia

---

[1] Brazil, Japan, Mexico, Nepal, Pakistan, the Philippines, Senegal, Togo and Ukraine are serving their second consecutive term.

SEBUTINDE (*Uganda*),*** Mr. Peter TOMKA (*Slovakia*),*** Ms. XUE Hanqin (*China*)*** and Mr. Abdulqawi Ahmed YUSUF (*Somalia*).**

---

* Term of office expires on 5 February 2024.

** Term of office expires on 5 February 2027.

*** Term of office expires on 5 February 2030.

75/404. Appointment of members of the Advisory Committee on Administrative and Budgetary Questions

At its 30th plenary meeting, on 23 November 2020, the General Assembly, on the recommendation of the Fifth Committee,[2] appointed the following persons as members of the Advisory Committee on Administrative and Budgetary Questions for a three-year term of office beginning on 1 January 2021: Mr. Abdallah Bachar Bong, Mr. Feliksas Bakanauskas, Mr. Pavel Chernikov, Ms. Donna-Marie Chiurazzi-Maxfield, Mr. Nabil Kalkoul, Ms. Julia A. Maciel, Ms. Vidisha Maitra, Ms. Caroline Nalwanga, Ms. Juliana Gaspar Ruas and Mr. Cihan Terzi.

As a result, as of 1 January 2021, the Advisory Committee on Administrative and Budgetary Questions is composed as follows: Mr. Yves Éric AHOUSSOUGBEMEY (*Benin*),* Mr. Amjad Qaid AL KUMAIM (*Yemen*),* Mr. Makiese Kinkela AUGUSTO (*Angola*),* Mr. Abdallah BACHAR BONG (*Chad*),*** Mr. Feliksas BAKANAUSKAS (*Lithuania*),*** Mr. Pavel CHERNIKOV (*Russian Federation*),*** Ms. Donna-Marie CHIURAZZI-MAXFIELD (*United States of America*),*** Mr. Patrick A. CHUASOTO (*Philippines*),** Mr. Udo Klaus FENCHEL (*Germany*),** Mr. Olivio FERMÍN (*Dominican Republic*),** Mr. Ihor HUMENNYI (*Ukraine*),* Mr. Conrod HUNTE (*Antigua and Barbuda*),* Mr. Marcel JULLIER (*Switzerland*),** Mr. Nabil KALKOUL (*Algeria*),*** Ms. Julia A. MACIEL (*Paraguay*),*** Ms. Vidisha MAITRA (*India*),*** Ms. Caroline NALWANGA (*Uganda*),*** Ms. Juliana Gaspar RUAS (*Brazil*),*** Ms. SUZUKI Yoriko (*Japan*),** Mr. Cihan TERZI (*Turkey*)*** and Mr. YE Xuenong (*China*).**

---

* Term of office expires on 31 December 2021.

** Term of office expires on 31 December 2022.

*** Term of office expires on 31 December 2023.

75/405. Appointment of members of the Committee on Contributions

At its 30th plenary meeting, on 23 November 2020, the General Assembly, on the recommendation of the Fifth Committee,[3] reappointed the following persons as members of the Committee on Contributions for a three-year term of office beginning on 1 January 2021: Mr. Michael Holtsch, Ms. Ji-sun Jun, Mr. Vadim Laputin, Mr. Henrique da Silveira Sardinha Pinto, Mr. Lin Shan and Mr. Steve Townley.

As a result, as of 1 January 2021, the Committee on Contributions is composed as follows: Mr. Syed Yawar ALI (*Pakistan*),* Mr. Jakub CHMIELEWSKI (*Poland*),* Mr. Cheikh Tidiane DÈME (*Senegal*),** Mr. Gordon ECKERSLEY (*Australia*),** Mr. Mohamed Mahmoud Ould EL GHAOUTH (*Mauritania*),** Mr. Bernardo GREIVER DEL HOYO (*Uruguay*),** Mr. Michael HOLTSCH (*Germany*),*** Ms. Ji-sun JUN (*Republic of Korea*),*** Mr. Vadim LAPUTIN (*Russian Federation*),*** Mr. LIN Shan (*China*),*** Mr. Robert Ngei MULE (*Kenya*),* Mr. OZAWA Toshiro (*Japan*),* Mr. Tõnis SAAR (*Estonia*),* Mr. Henrique da Silveira SARDINHA PINTO (*Brazil*),*** Mr. Brett Dennis SCHAEFER (*United States of America*),* Mr. Ugo SESSI (*Italy*),** Mr. Alejandro TORRES LÉPORI (*Argentina*)** and Mr. Steve TOWNLEY (*United Kingdom of Great Britain and Northern Ireland*).***

---

* Term of office expires on 31 December 2021.

** Term of office expires on 31 December 2022.

*** Term of office expires on 31 December 2023.

---

[2] A/75/579, para. 8.

[3] A/75/580, para. 4.

75/406. Confirmation of the appointment of members of the Investments Committee

At its 30th plenary meeting, on 23 November 2020, the General Assembly, on the recommendation of the Fifth Committee,[4] confirmed the appointment by the Secretary-General of the following persons as regular members of the Investments Committee for a three-year term of office beginning on 1 January 2021: Mr. Yasir O. Al-Rumayyan, Ms. Sarah Omotunde Alade, Ms. Natalia Khanjenkova and Ms. Patricia Parise.

At the same meeting, the General Assembly, on the recommendation of the Fifth Committee,[5] confirmed the selection by the Secretary-General of Mr. Michael Klein as Chair of the Investments Committee beginning on 1 January 2021.

At the same meeting, the General Assembly, on the recommendation of the Fifth Committee,[6] confirmed the reappointment by the Secretary-General of Mr. Macky Tall as an ad hoc member of the Investments Committee for a one-year term of office, beginning on 1 January 2021.

As a result, as of 1 January 2021, the Investments Committee is composed as follows: Mr. Michael KLEIN (*United States of America*, regular member and Chair),** Mr. Yasir O. AL-RUMAYYAN (*Saudi Arabia*, regular member),*** Ms. Sarah Omotunde ALADE (*Nigeria*, regular member),*** Ms. HONDA Keiko (*Japan*, regular member),* Mr. Simon JIANG (*China*, regular member),** Mr. Achim KASSOW (*Germany*, regular member),** Ms. Natalia KHANJENKOVA (*Russian Federation*, regular member),*** Ms. Patricia PARISE (*Argentina*, regular member),*** Ms. Luciane RIBEIRO (*Brazil*, regular member)** and Mr. Macky TALL (*Mali*, ad hoc member).*

---

*   Term of office expires on 31 December 2021.

**   Term of office expires on 31 December 2022.

***   Term of office expires on 31 December 2023.

75/407. Appointment of members of the International Civil Service Commission

At its 30th plenary meeting, on 23 November 2020, the General Assembly, on the recommendation of the Fifth Committee,[7] appointed the following persons as members of the International Civil Service Commission for a four-year term of office beginning on 1 January 2021: Mr. Larbi Djacta, Mr. Igor Golubovskiy, Mr. Pan-Suk Kim, Mr. Wang Xiaochu and Mr. El Hassane Zahid.

As a result, as of 1 January 2021, the International Civil Service Commission is composed as follows: Mr. Larbi DJACTA (*Algeria*, Chair),*** Mr. Aldo MANTOVANI (*Italy*, Vice-Chair),* Mr. Andrew Gbebay BANGALI (*Sierra Leone*),** Ms. Marie-Françoise BECHTEL (*France*),** Ms. Carleen GARDNER (*Jamaica*),** Mr. Igor GOLUBOVSKIY (*Russian Federation*),*** Mr. Luis Mariano HERMOSILLO SOSA (*Mexico*),* Mr. Pan-Suk KIM (*Republic of Korea*),*** Mr. KUMAMARU Yuji (*Japan*),* Mr. Ali KURER (*Libya*),** Mr. Jeffrey MOUNTS (*United States of America*),* Mr. Wolfgang STÖCKL (*Germany*),* Mr. WANG Xiaochu (*China*),*** Mr. Boguslaw WINID (*Poland*)** and Mr. El Hassane ZAHID (*Morocco*).***

---

*   Term of office expires on 31 December 2021.

**   Term of office expires on 31 December 2022.

***   Term of office expires on 31 December 2023.

---

[4] A/75/581, para. 4 (a).

[5] Ibid., para. 4 (b).

[6] Ibid., para. 4 (c).

[7] A/75/582, para. 5.

75/408. Appointment of members of the Independent Audit Advisory Committee

At its 30th plenary meeting, on 23 November 2020, the General Assembly, on the recommendation of the Fifth Committee,[8] appointed Ms. Janet St. Laurent as a member of the Independent Audit Advisory Committee for a three-year term of office beginning on 1 January 2021.

At its 48th (resumed) plenary meeting, on 31 December 2020, the General Assembly, on the recommendation of the Fifth Committee,[9] appointed Mr. Imran Vanker as a member of the Independent Audit Advisory Committee for a three-year term of office beginning on 1 January 2021.

As a result, as of 1 January 2021, the Independent Audit Advisory Committee is composed as follows: Ms. Dorothy BRADLEY (*Belize*),* Mr. Anton V. KOSYANENKO (*Russian Federation*),* Mr. Agus Joko PRAMONO (*Indonesia*),* Ms. Janet ST. LAURENT (*United States of America*)** and Mr. Imran VANKER (*South Africa*).**

---

*   Term of office expires on 31 December 2022.

**   Term of office expires on 31 December 2023.

75/409. Appointment of members and alternate members of the United Nations Staff Pension Committee

At its 30th plenary meeting, on 23 November 2020, the General Assembly, on the recommendation of the Fifth Committee,[10] appointed the following persons as members or alternate members of the United Nations Staff Pension Committee for a four-year term of office beginning on 1 January 2021: Mr. Ahmed Al Kabir, Mr. Dmitry S. Chumakov, Mr. Lovemore Mazemo, Mr. Philip Richard Okanda Owade, Ms. Pía Poroli, Mr. Jörg Stosberg, Mr. David Traystman and Mr. Yamaguchi Tomoya.

As a result, as of 1 January 2021, the members and alternate members of the United Nations Staff Pension Committee appointed by the General Assembly are as follows: Mr. Ahmed AL KABIR (*Bangladesh*), Mr. Dmitry S. CHUMAKOV (*Russian Federation*), Mr. Lovemore MAZEMO (*Zimbabwe*), Mr. Philip Richard Okanda OWADE (*Kenya*), Ms. Pía POROLI (*Argentina*), Mr. Jörg STOSBERG (*Germany*), Mr. David TRAYSTMAN (*United States of America*) and Mr. YAMAGUCHI Tomoya (*Japan*).

75/410. Election of members of the Committee for Programme and Coordination

At its 30th plenary meeting, on 23 November 2020, the General Assembly, on the basis of nominations by the Economic and Social Council[11] and in accordance with the annex to Council resolution 2008 (LX) of 14 May 1976 and Assembly decision 42/450 of 17 December 1987, elected ARMENIA, BELARUS, BRAZIL, CAMEROON, COSTA RICA, CUBA, ERITREA, ESWATINI, INDIA, IRAN (ISLAMIC REPUBLIC OF), ITALY, JAPAN, MALI, MALTA, PAKISTAN, POLAND, the UNITED KINGDOM OF GREAT BRITAIN AND NORTHERN IRELAND and the UNITED STATES OF AMERICA as members of the Committee for Programme and Coordination for a three-year term of office beginning on 1 January 2021 to fill the vacancies occurring on the expiration of the terms of office of BELARUS, BOTSWANA, BRAZIL, BULGARIA, BURKINA FASO, CAMEROON, CHAD, CHILE, CUBA, GERMANY, INDIA, IRAN (ISLAMIC REPUBLIC OF), ITALY, JAPAN, PAKISTAN, PORTUGAL, the REPUBLIC OF MOLDOVA, the UNITED KINGDOM OF GREAT BRITAIN AND NORTHERN IRELAND and the UNITED STATES OF AMERICA.

At its 48th plenary meeting, on 21 December 2020, the General Assembly, on the basis of the nomination by the Economic and Social Council[12] and in accordance with the annex to Council resolution 2008 (LX) and Assembly decision 42/450, elected GERMANY as a member of the Committee for Programme and Coordination for a three-year term of office beginning on 1 January 2021 and expiring on 31 December 2023.

---

[8] A/75/583, para. 4; see also A/75/PV.30.

[9] A/75/583/Add.1, para. 4.

[10] A/75/584, para. 4.

[11] See A/75/248; see also Economic and Social Council decision 2021/201 A.

[12] See A/75/248/Add.1; see also Economic and Social Council decision 2021/201 B.

As a result, as of 1 January 2021, the Committee for Programme and Coordination is composed of the following 31 Member States:[13] ANGOLA,* ARGENTINA,* ARMENIA,*** BELARUS,*** BRAZIL,*** CAMEROON,*** CHINA,** COMOROS,** COSTA RICA,*** CUBA,*** ERITREA,*** ESWATINI,*** ETHIOPIA,* FRANCE,* GERMANY,*** INDIA,*** IRAN (ISLAMIC REPUBLIC OF),*** ITALY,*** JAPAN,*** LIBERIA,** MALI,*** MALTA,*** MAURITANIA,** PAKISTAN,*** PARAGUAY,* POLAND,*** REPUBLIC OF KOREA,** RUSSIAN FEDERATION,* UNITED KINGDOM OF GREAT BRITAIN AND NORTHERN IRELAND,*** UNITED STATES OF AMERICA*** and URUGUAY.**

---

* Term of office expires on 31 December 2021.

** Term of office expires on 31 December 2022.

*** Term of office expires on 31 December 2023.

75/411. Election of the United Nations High Commissioner for Refugees

At its 30th plenary meeting, on 23 November 2020, the General Assembly, on the proposal of the Secretary-General,[14] re-elected Mr. Filippo GRANDI as United Nations High Commissioner for Refugees for a period of two and half years, beginning on 1 January 2021 and ending on 30 June 2023.

75/412. Appointment of members of the Committee on Conferences

At its 30th plenary meeting, on 23 November 2020, the General Assembly, in accordance with paragraph 2 of its resolution 43/222 B of 21 December 1988, took note of the appointment by its President, after consultations with the Chairs of the regional groups concerned, of FRANCE, KENYA, MALAYSIA, NIGERIA, the RUSSIAN FEDERATION and SRI LANKA as members of the Committee on Conferences for a three-year term of office beginning on 1 January 2021.

As a result, as of 1 January 2021, the Committee on Conferences is composed of the following 20 Member States:[15] ALGERIA,** AUSTRIA,** CHINA,** COMOROS,** ECUADOR,* FRANCE,*** GERMANY,* GHANA,* GUYANA,* IRAN (ISLAMIC REPUBLIC OF),* JAMAICA,** JAPAN,** KENYA,*** MALAYSIA,*** NIGERIA,*** RUSSIAN FEDERATION,*** SENEGAL,* SRI LANKA,*** UKRAINE* and UNITED STATES OF AMERICA.**

---

* Term of office expires on 31 December 2021.

** Term of office expires on 31 December 2022.

*** Term of office expires on 31 December 2023.

75/413. Election of members of the Organizational Committee of the Peacebuilding Commission

At its 44th plenary meeting, on 14 December 2020, the General Assembly, pursuant to its resolutions 60/180 of 20 December 2005, 60/261 of 8 May 2006 and 63/145 of 18 December 2008, elected BRAZIL, COSTA RICA, EGYPT, LEBANON and SOUTH AFRICA as members of the Organizational Committee of the Peacebuilding Commission for a two-year term of office beginning on 1 January 2021 to fill the vacancies occurring on the expiration of the terms of office of EGYPT, GUATEMALA, KENYA, MEXICO and NEPAL.

Pursuant to paragraphs 4 (a) to (d) of resolution 60/180, 25 States have already been elected and/or selected as members of the Organizational Committee of the Peacebuilding Commission: PERU and SLOVAKIA elected by the General Assembly;[16] CHINA, FRANCE, KENYA, RUSSIAN FEDERATION, SAINT VINCENT AND THE GRENADINES,

---

[13] One vacancy for a member from Western European and other States remains to be filled for a term of office beginning on the date of election and expiring on 31 December 2021; one vacancy for a member from Asia-Pacific States remains to be filled for a term of office beginning on the date of election and expiring on 31 December 2022; and one vacancy for a member from Latin American and Caribbean States remains to be filled for a term of office beginning on 1 January 2021 and expiring on 31 December 2023.

[14] A/75/338.

[15] One vacancy for a member from Latin American and Caribbean States remains to be filled for a term of office beginning on 1 January 2021 and expiring on 31 December 2023.

[16] See decision 74/413.

UNITED KINGDOM OF GREAT BRITAIN AND NORTHERN IRELAND and UNITED STATES OF AMERICA selected by the Security Council;[17] COLOMBIA, NIGERIA, NORWAY, REPUBLIC OF KOREA, SWITZERLAND and THAILAND elected by the Economic and Social Council;[18] CANADA, GERMANY, JAPAN, NETHERLANDS and SWEDEN selected by and from among the top 10 providers of assessed contributions to United Nations budgets and of voluntary contributions to United Nations funds, programmes and agencies, including a standing peacebuilding fund;[19] and BANGLADESH, ETHIOPIA, INDIA, PAKISTAN and RWANDA selected by and from among the top 10 providers of military personnel and civilian police to United Nations missions.[20]

As a result, on 1 January 2021, the Organizational Committee of the Peacebuilding Commission is composed of the following 30 Member States:[21] BANGLADESH,*** BRAZIL,*** CANADA,*** CHINA,* COLOMBIA,**** COSTA RICA,*** EGYPT,*** ETHIOPIA,*** FRANCE,* GERMANY,*** INDIA,*** JAPAN,*** KENYA,** LEBANON,*** NETHERLANDS,*** NIGERIA,**** NORWAY,**** PAKISTAN,*** PERU,** REPUBLIC OF KOREA,**** RUSSIAN FEDERATION,* RWANDA,*** SAINT VINCENT AND THE GRENADINES,** SLOVAKIA,** SOUTH AFRICA,*** SWEDEN,*** SWITZERLAND,**** THAILAND,**** UNITED KINGDOM OF GREAT BRITAIN AND NORTHERN IRELAND* and UNITED STATES OF AMERICA.*

---

*   Permanent members of the Security Council.

**   Term of office expires on 31 December 2021.

***   Term of office expires on 31 December 2022.

****   Term of office expires on 31 December 2022 or when they cease to be members of the Economic and Social Council, whichever comes earlier.

---

[17] See S/2021/21.

[18] See Economic and Social Council decisions 2021/201 A and B.

[19] See A/75/641.

[20] See A/75/640.

[21] One vacancy for the Economic and Social Council member from Eastern European States remains to be filled for a term of office beginning on the date of election in 2021 and expiring on 31 December 2022.

B.   Other decisions

1.   *Decisions adopted without reference to a Main Committee*

75/501.   Organization of the seventy-fifth session

At its 2nd plenary meeting, on 18 September 2020, the General Assembly, on the recommendation of the General Committee as set forth in its first report,[22] adopted a number of provisions concerning the organization of the seventy-fifth session.

At the same meeting, the General Assembly took note of the information provided in paragraph 44 of the same report of the General Committee concerning the conduct of the meetings of the plenary, including on the order and the format of statements.

Also at the same meeting, the General Assembly took note of the information provided in paragraph 53 of the same report of the General Committee concerning sponsorship of draft resolutions and decisions.

Also at the same meeting, the General Assembly took note of the information provided in paragraph 54 of the same report of the General Committee concerning rights of reply to addresses by Heads of State.

At its 30th plenary meeting, on 23 November 2020, the General Assembly, at the request of the Chair of the Second Committee, decided to extend the work of the Committee until Thursday, 10 December 2020.

At its 35th plenary meeting, on 2 December 2020, the General Assembly, on the proposal of its President, decided to postpone the date of recess of the seventy-fifth session of the Assembly from Monday, 14 December 2020, to Monday, 21 December 2020.

At the same meeting, the General Assembly, at the request of the Chair of the Fifth Committee, decided to extend the work of the Committee until Monday, 21 December 2020.

At its 46th plenary meeting, on 16 December 2020, the General Assembly, on the proposal of its President, decided to further postpone the date of recess of the seventy-fifth session of the Assembly from Monday, 21 December 2020, to Wednesday, 23 December 2020.

At the same meeting, the General Assembly, at the request of the Chair of the Fifth Committee, decided to further extend the work of the Committee until Wednesday, 23 December 2020.

75/502.   General debate of the seventy-fifth session of the General Assembly

At its 2nd plenary meeting, on 18 September 2020, the General Assembly, on the recommendation of the General Committee as set forth in its first report,[23] and taking note that, pursuant to resolution 57/301 of 13 March 2003, the general debate would begin on Tuesday, 22 September 2020, decided that the general debate would continue on Saturday, 26 September 2020, in order to maximize the number of speakers during that week.

75/503.   High-level meeting to commemorate the seventy-fifth anniversary of the United Nations

At its 2nd plenary meeting, on 18 September 2020, the General Assembly, on the recommendation of the General Committee as set forth in its first report,[24] decided, without setting a precedent, that, where physical presence was not practicable, a pre-recorded statement might be submitted by those who were invited to make opening statements at the high-level meeting to commemorate the seventy-fifth anniversary of the United Nations, to be held pursuant to resolution 73/299 of 14 June 2019.

---

[22] A/75/250.

[23] Ibid., para. 38.

[24] Ibid., para. 44.

75/504. Adoption of the agenda and allocation of agenda items

At its 2nd plenary meeting, on 18 September 2020, the General Assembly, on the recommendation of the General Committee as set forth in its first report,[25] adopted the agenda[26] and the allocation of agenda items[27] for the seventy-fifth session.

At the same meeting, the General Assembly, on the recommendation of the General Committee as set forth in its first report,[28] decided to include in the agenda of its seventy-fifth session the item entitled "Question of the Comorian island of Mayotte", under heading B (Maintenance of international peace and security), on the understanding that there would be no consideration of this item by the Assembly.

Also at the same meeting, the General Assembly, on the recommendation of the General Committee as set forth in its first report,[29] decided to defer consideration of the item entitled "Question of the Malagasy islands of Glorieuses, Juan de Nova, Europa and Bassas da India" and to include it in the provisional agenda of its seventy-sixth session.

Also at the same meeting, the General Assembly, on the recommendation of the General Committee as set forth in its first report,[30] decided to include in the agenda of its seventy-fifth session the item entitled "The situation in the temporarily occupied territories of Ukraine" under heading B (Maintenance of international peace and security).

Also at the same meeting, the General Assembly, on the recommendation of the General Committee as set forth in its first report,[31] by a recorded vote of 101 to 13, with 22 abstentions,[32] decided to include in the agenda of its seventy-fifth session the item entitled "The responsibility to protect and the prevention of genocide, war crimes, ethnic cleansing and crimes against humanity" under heading I (Organizational, administrative and other matters).

At its 30th plenary meeting, on 23 November 2020, the General Assembly decided to consider directly in plenary meeting agenda item 25 entitled "Operational activities for development", under heading A (Promotion of sustained economic growth and sustainable development in accordance with the relevant resolutions of the General Assembly and recent United Nations conferences), and to proceed expeditiously with the consideration of a draft decision.[33]

75/505. High-level meeting of the General Assembly to commemorate the seventy-fifth anniversary of the United Nations

At its 15th plenary meeting, on 29 September 2020, the General Assembly, on the proposal of its President,[34] noting with concern the situation regarding the coronavirus disease (COVID-19) pandemic and the limitations recommended on meetings within the United Nations premises as precautionary measures aimed at containing the spread of COVID-19, and recalling its resolution 73/299 of 14 June 2019 and its decision 74/562 of 22 July 2020:

(a)   Decided, without setting a precedent for future mandated high-level meetings planned for future high-level weeks, that entities and organizations having received a standing invitation to participate as observers in the sessions and the work of the General Assembly, other than the European Union, could each submit a pre-recorded statement of their high officials, which would be played in the General Assembly Hall during the high-level meeting of the Assembly to commemorate the seventy-fifth anniversary of the United Nations, after introduction by their representative who was physically present in the Assembly Hall;

---

[25] Ibid., paras. 89–120.

[26] A/75/251.

[27] A/75/252.

[28] A/75/250, para. 97.

[29] Ibid., para. 98.

[30] Ibid., para. 99.

[31] Ibid., para. 105.

[32] See A/75/PV.2.

[33] A/75/L.26.

[34] A/75/L.2.

(b)   Also decided that, in addition to the verbatim records of the high-level meeting, the President of the General Assembly would circulate as a document of the Assembly a compilation document of the statements delivered by observers of the General Assembly referred to in paragraph (a) above by means of pre-recorded statements during the high-level meeting and submitted to the President no later than the day on which the pre-recorded statement was played in the Assembly Hall.

75/506. Introduction of certain reports in the plenary meetings at the seventy-fifth session of the General Assembly

At its 16th plenary meeting, on 13 October 2020, the General Assembly, on the proposal of its President,[35] noting with concern the situation regarding the coronavirus disease (COVID-19) pandemic, and noting that there were certain limitations in place on access to the United Nations premises as precautionary measures aimed at containing the spread of COVID-19, including quarantine requirements:

(a)   Decided, without setting a precedent for future plenary meetings of the General Assembly, that, during the seventy-fifth session, where quarantine requirements were in place, those who were invited to introduce reports under the agenda items entitled "Report of the Human Rights Council", "Report of the International Court of Justice", "Report of the International Criminal Court", "Report of the International Atomic Energy Agency", "Cooperation between the United Nations and regional and other organizations" and "International Residual Mechanism for Criminal Tribunals" might each submit a pre-recorded statement, which would be played in the General Assembly Hall after the introduction by the President of the General Assembly at the plenary meetings concerned;

(b)   Also decided that, in addition to the verbatim records of the plenary meetings, the President of the General Assembly would circulate, as a document of the Assembly, each statement delivered by those who were invited to introduce reports under the agenda items referred to in paragraph (a) above by means of pre-recorded statement, which would be attached to the verbatim records of the meeting.

75/507. Report of the International Residual Mechanism for Criminal Tribunals

At its 17th plenary meeting, on 21 October 2020, the General Assembly took note of the eighth annual report of the International Residual Mechanism for Criminal Tribunals.[36]

75/508. Report of the International Court of Justice

At its 20th plenary meeting, on 3 November 2020, the General Assembly took note of the report of the International Court of Justice.[37]

75/509. Report of the Economic and Social Council

At its 21st plenary meeting, on 5 November 2020, the General Assembly took note of the report of the Economic and Social Council.[38]

75/510. Procedure for decision-making in the General Assembly[39] when an in-person meeting is not possible

At its 26th plenary meeting, on 13 November 2020, the General Assembly, on the proposal of Andorra, Austria, Barbados, Belgium, Canada, Colombia, Costa Rica, Croatia, Cyprus, Denmark, the Dominican Republic, Ecuador, Estonia, Finland, the Gambia, Georgia, Ghana, Honduras, Hungary, Iceland, Ireland, Jamaica, Latvia, Lebanon, Liechtenstein, Lithuania, Luxembourg, Malta, Mexico, Monaco, the Netherlands, New Zealand, Nigeria, Norway, Oman, Panama, Peru, the Philippines, Qatar, the Republic of Korea, San Marino, Sierra Leone, Sweden, Switzerland

---

[35] A/75/L.3.

[36] A/75/276-S/2020/763.

[37] *Official Records of the General Assembly, Seventy-fifth Session, Supplement No. 4* (A/75/4).

[38] Ibid., *Supplement No.3* (A/75/3/Rev.1).

[39] The subsidiary organs of the General Assembly may apply the procedure set out in the present decision.

and Ukraine,[40] by a recorded vote of 123 to 19, with 29 abstentions,[41] reaffirming that the procedure for adopting proposals in the General Assembly was governed by the provisions of the Charter of the United Nations, the rules of procedure of the General Assembly and other applicable resolutions and decisions of the General Assembly, and stressing that the present decision was without prejudice to any future discussion on the rules of procedure; recalling the unprecedented limitations caused by the coronavirus disease (COVID-19) pandemic, when in-person meetings of the General Assembly were not possible owing to precautionary measures aimed at containing the spread of COVID-19; determined to ensure the full functionality of the General Assembly at all times; reaffirming that the General Assembly shall, as a rule and in accordance with established practice, always meet in person, and recognizing that exception to that practice shall be made only in the most extraordinary circumstances and for as limited a time period as possible; acknowledging that such circumstances called for increased coordination by the President of the General Assembly with Member States, and reaffirming that the procedure set out in the present decision shall be applied in as limited a manner as possible and with a particular focus on the continuity of essential functions of the General Assembly; and stressing the importance of orderly, transparent and inclusive consultations, in particular in the absence of in-person meetings, with a view to establishing the broadest possible agreement on proposals put before the General Assembly for action:

(a)   Decided that the procedure set out in the present decision shall strictly apply without discrimination and only in the most exceptional circumstances, when an in-person meeting of the General Assembly was not possible for a prolonged period of time owing to concrete and ongoing risks to the safety and well-being of representatives of Member States and United Nations personnel;

(b)   Also decided that the President of the General Assembly shall determine that the circumstances described in paragraph (a) above apply, after consultation with the Chairs of the Main Committees and guided by the recommendation of the Secretary-General, in consultation with the Medical Director, the head of the Department of Safety and Security of the Secretariat and the host State authorities, as relevant and applicable to the situation, and further decided that such determination shall immediately be communicated to Member States, reviewed constantly and considered revoked upon convening the first in-person meeting following the application of the procedure prescribed in the present decision;

(c)   Authorized the President of the General Assembly, where an in-person meeting of the General Assembly was not possible, to circulate, upon request by the main sponsor, a proposal that had been issued as a document of the General Assembly in all official languages to all Member States, with a view to taking action thereon;

(d)   Decided that the President of the General Assembly shall put the proposal in question under a silence procedure of 72 hours, and decided that, if the silence was not broken, the resolution or decision shall be considered adopted;

(e)   Also decided that the President of the General Assembly shall put a proposal to the vote without holding an in-person meeting only in the event that a vote was requested by a Member State in writing during the silence procedure under paragraph (d) above or if the silence was broken by means other than a request for a vote;

(f)   Further decided that the General Assembly shall take note of proposals adopted by means of silence procedure at its first plenary meeting held when in-person meetings were possible;

(g)   Decided that the President of the General Assembly shall put a proposal to the vote in accordance with the arrangements set out below:

(i)   The President shall circulate a letter to all Member States announcing that a vote had been requested on a specific proposal and indicating the date and time at which the vote would commence; such a date and time shall be fixed in a manner that would allow at least 72 hours between the circulation of the letter by the President and the commencement of the vote, except for procedural motions, which shall be put to the vote within 24 hours of the time of circulation of the President's letter; the letter shall be accompanied by the proposal in question, which shall be in the six official languages of the General Assembly;

---

[40] A/75/L.7/Rev.1 and A/75/L.7/Rev.1/Add.1.

[41] See A/75/PV.26.

(ii)   No other action might be proposed in relation to the proposal after a vote on the proposal had commenced at the date and time announced by the President, except a point of order in connection with the actual conduct of the voting; this did not prevent the General Assembly from taking decisions on other proposals in parallel;

(iii)   Member States might vote "in favour" or "against" or indicate "abstain" through an electronic means provided by the Secretariat within existing resources and specified by the President before the voting period, which shall be one hour; the votes cast by Member States shall become visible to other Member States five minutes before the closure of the voting period;

(iv)   The voting process shall be considered valid if a majority of the members of the General Assembly were present during the voting process, which shall be determined by counting those Member States that had affirmed their presence during the voting period before accessing the electronic voting page for the proposal concerned;

(v)   If the votes in favour reached the required majority, the proposal shall be considered adopted and the General Assembly would be informed of the decision at its first plenary meeting held after the cessation of the precautionary measures as soon as the circumstances allowed;

(h)   Authorized the President of the General Assembly, in the event that an amendment or a procedural motion was proposed at least 24 hours in advance of the original date and time of the vote on a proposal announced in the letter of the President pursuant to paragraph (g) (i) above, to immediately suspend the scheduled vote and immediately circulate the amendment or the procedural motion in question, and take one of the following steps:

(i)   If an amendment was proposed, the President shall circulate the amendment to all Member States; the amendment might be placed under a silence procedure or, if a vote was requested, shall be put to the vote in accordance with paragraph (g) above;

(ii)   The President shall put the procedural motion in question to the vote in accordance with the relevant rules of procedure of the General Assembly and paragraph (g) above;

(i)   Decided that if a point of order was raised during the voting period referred to in paragraph (g) (iii) above in connection with the actual conduct of the voting in accordance with rule 88 of the rules of procedure of the General Assembly, the President of the General Assembly shall suspend the vote and apply the following procedure:

(i)   The point of order shall be decided by the President in accordance with rule 71 of the rules of procedure; the President's ruling would be communicated by the President to all Member States, indicating the time by which Member States might appeal against the ruling of the President, which shall be one hour from the time at which the communication was sent out;

(ii)   If there was no appeal against the ruling during the specified time frame, the President's ruling shall stand;

(iii)   In the event of an appeal, the President would immediately notify all Member States that an appeal had been made to the President's ruling and indicate the date and time of the voting on the appeal, which shall take place within one hour of the time when the President had notified that an appeal had been made to the ruling; the voting shall be held in accordance with paragraphs (g) (ii) to (v) above;

(iv)   The President would communicate a new date and time at which the voting process on the underlying proposal would resume;

(j)   Also decided that the Secretariat shall, as part of its intergovernmental services and within existing resources, provide technical support and assistance upon request by Member States to ensure the full and equal access by all States to the procedure outlined in the present decision.

75/511. United Nations Pledging Conference for Development Activities

At its 30th plenary meeting, on 23 November 2020, the General Assembly, on the proposal of its President,[42] recalling its resolution 45/215 of 21 December 1990, in which it had decided that the United Nations Pledging Conference for Development Activities would continue to be convened early in November, noting that currently there were certain limitations in place on the use of the United Nations premises as precautionary measures aimed at

---

[42] A/75/L.26.

containing the spread of the coronavirus disease (COVID-19), and reaffirming its resolution 74/303 of 4 September 2020, in which it had underlined the need to further enhance the role, authority, effectiveness and efficiency of the General Assembly to address the evolving global challenges, decided to postpone the Pledging Conference to early 2021.

75/542. Investigation into the conditions and circumstances resulting in the tragic death of Dag Hammarskjöld and of the members of the party accompanying him

At its 47th plenary meeting, on 21 December 2020, the General Assembly, on the proposal of Sweden,[43] recalling its resolution 74/248 of 27 December 2019, in which it had requested the Secretary-General to reappoint the Eminent Person appointed pursuant to General Assembly resolution 72/252 of 24 December 2017 to continue to review the information received and possible new information made available by Member States, including by individuals and private entities, to assess its probative value and to draw conclusions from the investigations already conducted, and to report to the Assembly before the end of its seventy-fifth session on progress made, noting with concern the situation concerning the coronavirus disease (COVID-19) pandemic and the challenges that it posed for Member States, individuals and private entities, and taking note of the letter dated 5 November 2020 from the Secretary-General addressed to the President of the General Assembly:[44]

(a) Requested the Secretary-General to report to the General Assembly before the end of the seventy-sixth session on progress made;

(b) Decided to include in the provisional agenda of its seventy-seventh session the item entitled "Investigation into the conditions and circumstances resulting in the tragic death of Dag Hammarskjöld and of the members of the party accompanying him".

75/554. Agenda items remaining for consideration by the General Assembly at its seventy-fifth session

At its 48th (resumed) plenary meeting, on 31 December 2020, the General Assembly, apart from organizational matters and items that might have to be considered by operation of the rules of procedure of the Assembly, took note of the following agenda items that remained for consideration during its seventy-fifth session:

Item 9.　Report of the Economic and Social Council

Item 10.　Implementation of the Declaration of Commitment on HIV/AIDS and the political declarations on HIV/AIDS

Item 11.　Sport for development and peace:

(a) Sport for development and peace

(b) Building a peaceful and better world through sport and the Olympic ideal

Item 12.　Improving global road safety

Item 13.　2001–2010: Decade to Roll Back Malaria in Developing Countries, Particularly in Africa

Item 14.　Integrated and coordinated implementation of and follow-up to the outcomes of the major United Nations conferences and summits in the economic, social and related fields

Item 15.　Culture of peace

Item 19.　Sustainable development

Item 23.　Groups of countries in special situations:

(a) Follow-up to the Fourth United Nations Conference on the Least Developed Countries

---

[43] A/75/L.49.

[44] A/75/635.

Item 29. Space as a driver of sustainable development

Item 30. Report of the Security Council

Item 31. Report of the Peacebuilding Commission

Item 32. Elimination of unilateral extraterritorial coercive economic measures as a means of political and economic compulsion

Item 33. The role of diamonds in fuelling conflict

Item 34. Prevention of armed conflict:

    (a) Prevention of armed conflict

    (b) Strengthening the role of mediation in the peaceful settlement of disputes, conflict prevention and resolution

Item 35. Protracted conflicts in the GUAM area and their implications for international peace, security and development

Item 36. Zone of peace and cooperation of the South Atlantic

Item 37. The situation in the Middle East

Item 38. Question of Palestine

Item 40. The situation in the occupied territories of Azerbaijan

Item 41. Question of the Comorian island of Mayotte

Item 42. Necessity of ending the economic, commercial and financial embargo imposed by the United States of America against Cuba

Item 43. The situation in Central America: progress in fashioning a region of peace, freedom, democracy and development

Item 44. Question of Cyprus

Item 45. Armed aggression against the Democratic Republic of the Congo

Item 46. Question of the Falkland Islands (Malvinas)

Item 47. The situation of democracy and human rights in Haiti

Item 48. Armed Israeli aggression against the Iraqi nuclear installations and its grave consequences for the established international system concerning the peaceful uses of nuclear energy, the non-proliferation of nuclear weapons and international peace and security

Item 49. Consequences of the Iraqi occupation of and aggression against Kuwait

Item 54. Comprehensive review of the whole question of peacekeeping operations in all their aspects

Item 56. Questions relating to information

Item 64. Peacebuilding and sustaining peace

Item 65. The situation in the temporarily occupied territories of Ukraine

Item 66. New Partnership for Africa's Development: progress in implementation and international support:

    (a) New Partnership for Africa's Development: progress in implementation and international support

    (b) Causes of conflict and the promotion of durable peace and sustainable development in Africa

Item 70. Elimination of racism, racial discrimination, xenophobia and related intolerance:

    (b) Comprehensive implementation of and follow-up to the Durban Declaration and Programme of Action

Item 73. Strengthening of the coordination of humanitarian and disaster relief assistance of the United Nations, including special economic assistance:

    (a) Strengthening of the coordination of emergency humanitarian assistance of the United Nations

    (b) Assistance to the Palestinian people

    (c) Special economic assistance to individual countries or regions

    (d) Strengthening of international cooperation and coordination of efforts to study, mitigate and minimize the consequences of the Chernobyl disaster

Item 76. Oceans and the law of the sea:

    (a) Oceans and the law of the sea

Item 91. Request for an advisory opinion of the International Court of Justice on the legal consequences of the separation of the Chagos Archipelago from Mauritius in 1965

Item 92. Extraordinary Chambers in the Courts of Cambodia – residual functions

Item 98. Developments in the field of information and telecommunications in the context of international security

Item 103. General and complete disarmament

Item 111. Crime prevention and criminal justice

Item 112. Countering the use of information and communications technologies for criminal purposes

Item 115. Report of the Secretary-General on the work of the Organization

Item 116. Report of the Secretary-General on the Peacebuilding Fund

Item 117. Notification by the Secretary-General under Article 12, paragraph 2, of the Charter of the United Nations

Item 118. Elections to fill vacancies in principal organs:

    (a) Election of non-permanent members of the Security Council

    (b) Election of members of the Economic and Social Council

Item 119. Elections to fill vacancies in subsidiary organs and other elections:

    (a) Election of members of the Committee for Programme and Coordination

Item 120. Appointments to fill vacancies in subsidiary organs and other appointments:

    (g) Appointment of members of the Committee on Conferences

    (h) Appointment of members of the Joint Inspection Unit

    (i) Appointment of members of the Board of the 10-Year Framework of Programmes on Sustainable Consumption and Production Patterns

    (j) Confirmation of the appointment of the Administrator of the United Nations Development Programme

    (k) Confirmation of the appointment of the Secretary-General of the United Nations Conference on Trade and Development

Item 121.   Admission of new Members to the United Nations

Item 122.   Follow-up to the outcome of the Millennium Summit

Item 123.   The United Nations Global Counter-Terrorism Strategy

Item 124.   Commemoration of the abolition of slavery and the transatlantic slave trade

Item 125.   Implementation of the resolutions of the United Nations

Item 126.   Revitalization of the work of the General Assembly

Item 127.   Question of equitable representation on and increase in the membership of the Security Council and other matters related to the Security Council

Item 128.   Strengthening of the United Nations system:

    (a)   Strengthening of the United Nations system

    (b)   Central role of the United Nations system in global governance

Item 129.   Multilingualism

Item 130.   Cooperation between the United Nations and regional and other organizations:

    (a)   Cooperation between the United Nations and the African Union

    (c)   Cooperation between the United Nations and the Asian-African Legal Consultative Organization

    (f)   Cooperation between the United Nations and the Organization of American States

    (g)   Cooperation between the United Nations and the Organization for Security and Cooperation in Europe

    (h)   Cooperation between the United Nations and the Caribbean Community

    (i)   Cooperation between the United Nations and the Economic Cooperation Organization

    (j)   Cooperation between the United Nations and the International Organization of la Francophonie

    (l)   Cooperation between the United Nations and the Council of Europe

    (m)   Cooperation between the United Nations and the Economic Community of Central African States

    (n)   Cooperation between the United Nations and the Organisation for the Prohibition of Chemical Weapons

    (p)   Cooperation between the United Nations and the Pacific Islands Forum

    (r)   Cooperation between the United Nations and the Community of Portuguese-speaking Countries

    (s)   Cooperation between the United Nations and the Shanghai Cooperation Organization

    (t)   Cooperation between the United Nations and the Collective Security Treaty Organization

    (x)   Cooperation between the United Nations and the International Organization for Migration

    (z)   Cooperation between the United Nations and the International Fund for Saving the Aral Sea

    (aa)   Cooperation between the United Nations and the Organization for Economic Cooperation and Development

Item 131. Global health and foreign policy

Item 134. Sexual exploitation and abuse: implementing a zero-tolerance policy

Item 135. The responsibility to protect and the prevention of genocide, war crimes, ethnic cleansing and crimes against humanity

Item 136. Impact of rapid technological change on the achievement of the Sustainable Development Goals and targets

Item 138. Financial reports and audited financial statements, and reports of the Board of Auditors:

    (a)   United Nations

    (b)   United Nations peacekeeping operations

    (c)   International Trade Centre

    (d)   United Nations University

    (e)   United Nations Development Programme

    (f)   United Nations Capital Development Fund

    (g)   United Nations Children's Fund

    (h)   United Nations Relief and Works Agency for Palestine Refugees in the Near East

    (i)   United Nations Institute for Training and Research

    (j)   Voluntary funds administered by the United Nations High Commissioner for Refugees

    (k)   Fund of the United Nations Environment Programme

    (l)   United Nations Population Fund

    (m) United Nations Human Settlements Programme

    (n)   United Nations Office on Drugs and Crime

    (o)   United Nations Office for Project Services

    (p)   United Nations Entity for Gender Equality and the Empowerment of Women (UN-Women)

    (q)   International Residual Mechanism for Criminal Tribunals

    (r)   United Nations Joint Staff Pension Fund

Item 139. Review of the efficiency of the administrative and financial functioning of the United Nations

Item 140. Programme budget for 2020

Item 141. Programme budget for 2021

Item 142. Programme planning

Item 143. Improving the financial situation of the United Nations

Item 144. Pattern of conferences

Item 145. Scale of assessments for the apportionment of the expenses of the United Nations

Item 146. Human resources management

Item 147. Joint Inspection Unit

Item 148. United Nations common system

Item 149. United Nations pension system

Item 150. Administrative and budgetary coordination of the United Nations with the specialized agencies and the International Atomic Energy Agency

Item 151. Report on the activities of the Office of Internal Oversight Services

Item 152. Administration of justice at the United Nations

Item 153. Financing of the International Residual Mechanism for Criminal Tribunals

Item 154. Administrative and budgetary aspects of the financing of the United Nations peacekeeping operations

Item 155. Financing of the United Nations Interim Security Force for Abyei

Item 156. Financing of the United Nations Multidimensional Integrated Stabilization Mission in the Central African Republic

Item 157. Financing of the United Nations Operation in Côte d'Ivoire

Item 158. Financing of the United Nations Peacekeeping Force in Cyprus

Item 159. Financing of the United Nations Organization Stabilization Mission in the Democratic Republic of the Congo

Item 160. Financing of the United Nations Mission in East Timor

Item 161. Financing of the United Nations Stabilization Mission in Haiti

Item 162. Financing of the United Nations Mission for Justice Support in Haiti

Item 163. Financing of the United Nations Interim Administration Mission in Kosovo

Item 164. Financing of the United Nations Mission in Liberia

Item 165. Financing of the United Nations Multidimensional Integrated Stabilization Mission in Mali

Item 166. Financing of the United Nations peacekeeping forces in the Middle East:

    (a) United Nations Disengagement Observer Force

    (b) United Nations Interim Force in Lebanon

Item 167. Financing of the United Nations Mission in South Sudan

Item 168. Financing of the United Nations Mission for the Referendum in Western Sahara

Item 169. Financing of the African Union-United Nations Hybrid Operation in Darfur

Item 170. Financing of the activities arising from Security Council resolution 1863 (2009)

Item 171. Report of the Committee on Relations with the Host Country

2. *Decisions adopted on the reports of the First Committee*

75/512. Reduction of military budgets

At its 37th plenary meeting, on 7 December 2020, the General Assembly took note of the report of the First Committee.[45]

---

[45] A/75/390.

75/513. Maintenance of international security – good-neighbourliness, stability and development in South-Eastern Europe

At its 37th plenary meeting, on 7 December 2020, the General Assembly, on the recommendation of the First Committee,[46] decided to include in the provisional agenda of its seventy-seventh session the item entitled "Maintenance of international security – good-neighbourliness, stability and development in South-Eastern Europe".

75/514. Further practical measures for the prevention of an arms race in outer space

At its 37th plenary meeting, on 7 December 2020, the General Assembly, by a recorded vote of 152 to 3, with 30 abstentions,[47] on the recommendation of the First Committee,[48] recalling its resolution 74/34 of 12 December 2019 and other resolutions on this matter, decided to include in the provisional agenda of its seventy-sixth session, under the item entitled "Prevention of an arms race in outer space", the sub-item entitled "Further practical measures for the prevention of an arms race in outer space".

75/515. Treaty banning the production of fissile material for nuclear weapons or other nuclear explosive devices

At its 37th plenary meeting, on 7 December 2020, the General Assembly, by a recorded vote of 184 to 1, with 4 abstentions,[49] on the recommendation of the First Committee,[50] recalling its decision 74/509 of 12 December 2019, decided to include in the provisional agenda of its seventy-sixth session, under the item entitled "General and complete disarmament", the sub-item entitled "Treaty banning the production of fissile material for nuclear weapons or other nuclear explosive devices".

75/516. Nuclear disarmament verification

At its 37th plenary meeting, on 7 December 2020, the General Assembly, by a recorded vote of 184 to 1, with 2 abstentions,[51] on the recommendation of the First Committee,[52] recalling its resolutions 71/67 of 5 December 2016 and 74/50 of 12 December 2019 and its decisions 72/514 of 4 December 2017 and 73/514 of 5 December 2018, decided to include in the provisional agenda of its seventy-sixth session, under the item entitled "General and complete disarmament", the sub-item entitled "Nuclear disarmament verification".

75/517. Compliance with non-proliferation, arms limitation and disarmament agreements and commitments

At its 37th plenary meeting, on 7 December 2020, the General Assembly, by a recorded vote of 177 to 1, with 9 abstentions,[53] on the recommendation of the First Committee,[54] recalling its resolution 72/32 of 4 December 2017 and previous resolutions on this matter, decided to include in the provisional agenda of its seventy-sixth session, under the item entitled "General and complete disarmament", the sub-item entitled "Compliance with non-proliferation, arms limitation and disarmament agreements and commitments".

---

[46] A/75/393, para. 7.

[47] See A/75/PV.37.

[48] A/75/397, para.16.

[49] See A/75/PV.37.

[50] A/75/399, para. 97.

[51] See A/75/PV.37.

[52] A/75/399, para. 97.

[53] See A/75/PV.37.

[54] A/75/399, para. 97.

75/518. Missiles

At its 37th plenary meeting, on 7 December 2020, the General Assembly, by a recorded vote of 174 to 3, with 6 abstentions,[55] on the recommendation of the First Committee,[56] recalling its resolutions 54/54 F of 1 December 1999, 55/33 A of 20 November 2000, 56/24 B of 29 November 2001, 57/71 of 22 November 2002, 58/37 of 8 December 2003, 59/67 of 3 December 2004, 61/59 of 6 December 2006 and 63/55 of 2 December 2008 and its decisions 60/515 of 8 December 2005, 62/514 of 5 December 2007, 65/517 of 8 December 2010, 66/516 of 2 December 2011, 67/516 of 3 December 2012, 68/517 of 5 December 2013, 69/517 of 2 December 2014, 71/516 of 5 December 2016 and 73/513 of 5 December 2018, decided to include in the provisional agenda of its seventy-seventh session, under the item entitled "General and complete disarmament", the sub-item entitled "Missiles".

75/519. Disarmament Commission

At its 37th plenary meeting, on 7 December 2020, the General Assembly, on the recommendation of the First Committee,[57] recalling its decisions 74/511 of 12 December 2019 and 74/546 of 2 April 2020, and noting with concern the situation concerning the coronavirus disease (COVID-19), decided:

(a)   That the Disarmament Commission shall hold a substantive session for a period not exceeding three weeks during 2021, namely from 5 to 23 April, and submit a substantive report to the General Assembly at its seventy-sixth session;

(b)   That the Disarmament Commission shall hold its organizational session at the beginning of 2021, before the substantive session, to elect its Bureau and address other outstanding organizational matters;

(c)   To include in the provisional agenda of its seventy-sixth session, under the item entitled "Review of the implementation of the recommendations and decisions adopted by the General Assembly at its tenth special session", the sub-item entitled "Report of the Disarmament Commission".

75/520. Provisional programme of work and timetable of the First Committee for 2021

At its 37th plenary meeting, on 7 December 2020, the General Assembly, on the recommendation of the First Committee,[58] approved the provisional programme of work and timetable of the Committee for 2021, as set out in the annex to the report of the Committee.[59]

75/521. Programme planning (First Committee)

At its 37th plenary meeting, on 7 December 2020, the General Assembly took note of the report of the First Committee.[60]

75/550. Open-ended Working Group on Developments in the Field of Information and Telecommunications in the Context of International Security established pursuant to General Assembly resolution 73/27 of 5 December 2018

At its 48th (resumed) plenary meeting, on 31 December 2020, the General Assembly, on the recommendation of the First Committee,[61] recalling its resolutions 73/27 of 5 December 2018 and 74/29 of 12 December 2019, noting

---

[55] See A/75/PV.37.

[56] A/75/399, para. 97.

[57] A/75/401, para. 17.

[58] A/75/407, para. 5.

[59] A/75/407.

[60] A/75/408.

[61] A/75/394, para. 18.

that the Open-ended Working Group on Developments in the Field of Information and Telecommunications in the Context of International Security had held its organizational and first and second substantive sessions in 2019 and 2020, and noting also that, owing to the coronavirus disease (COVID-19) pandemic, the third and final substantive session, scheduled for 6 to 10 July 2020, had been cancelled, decided that the Open-ended Working Group, while continuing its current work pursuant to its mandate under resolution 73/27, shall convene its third and final substantive session from 8 to 12 March 2021.

75/551. Group of Governmental Experts on Advancing Responsible State Behaviour in Cyberspace in the Context of International Security established pursuant to General Assembly resolution 73/266 of 22 December 2018

At its 48th (resumed) plenary meeting, on 31 December 2020, the General Assembly, on the recommendation of the First Committee,[62] recalling its resolutions 73/266 of 22 December 2018 and 74/28 of 12 December 2019, noting that the Secretary-General had convened the first and second sessions of the Group of Governmental Experts on Advancing Responsible State Behaviour in Cyberspace in the Context of International Security in 2019 and 2020, and noting with concern that, owing to the coronavirus disease (COVID-19) pandemic, the third session of the Group of Governmental Experts, scheduled for 17 to 21 August 2020, could not take place, decided to request the Secretary-General to convene the third session and the fourth and final session of the Group before the end of May 2021.

75/552. Problems arising from the accumulation of conventional ammunition stockpiles in surplus

At its 48th (resumed) plenary meeting, on 31 December 2020, the General Assembly, on the recommendation of the First Committee,[63] recalling its decision 59/515 of 3 December 2004 and its resolutions 60/74 of 8 December 2005 and 61/72 of 6 December 2006, its resolution 63/61 of 2 December 2008, by which it had welcomed the report of the Group of Governmental Experts established pursuant to resolution 61/72 to consider further steps to enhance cooperation with regard to the issue of conventional ammunition stockpiles in surplus, and its resolutions 64/51 of 2 December 2009, 66/42 of 2 December 2011, 68/52 of 5 December 2013, 70/35 of 7 December 2015, 72/55 of 4 December 2017 and 74/65 of 12 December 2019, acknowledging the impact of the coronavirus disease (COVID-19) on the convening of meetings within United Nations premises, taking note of the impact of COVID-19 on the ability of the Group of Governmental Experts on problems arising from the accumulation of conventional ammunition stockpiles in surplus, established pursuant to resolution 72/55, to convene for 10 of its working days, as scheduled, and recalling the request to the Secretary-General contained in resolution 74/65 to report to the General Assembly on the work of the Group upon its completion, decided to request the Secretary-General to convene the Group of Governmental Experts for up to 10 working days in 2021 to enable the Group to complete its work, and also decided to include in the provisional agenda of its seventy-sixth session, under the item entitled "General and complete disarmament", the sub-item entitled "Problems arising from the accumulation of conventional ammunition stockpiles in surplus".

3. *Decisions adopted on the reports of the Special Political and Decolonization Committee (Fourth Committee)*

75/522. Comprehensive review of the whole question of peacekeeping operations in all their aspects

At its 41st plenary meeting, on 10 December 2020, the General Assembly took note of the report of the Special Political and Decolonization Committee (Fourth Committee).[64]

---

[62] A/75/394, para. 18.

[63] A/75/399, para. 97.

[64] A/75/413.

75/523. Question of Gibraltar

At its 41st plenary meeting, on 10 December 2020, the General Assembly, on the recommendation of the Special Political and Decolonization Committee (Fourth Committee),[65] recalling its decision 74/515 of 13 December 2019:

(a) Urged the Governments of Spain and the United Kingdom of Great Britain and Northern Ireland, while listening to the interests and aspirations of Gibraltar that were legitimate under international law, to reach, in the spirit of the Brussels Declaration of 27 November 1984, a definitive solution to the question of Gibraltar, in the light of the relevant resolutions of the General Assembly and applicable principles, and in the spirit of the Charter of the United Nations;

(b) Took note of the desire of the United Kingdom to continue with the trilateral Forum for Dialogue;

(c) Took note of the position of Spain that the trilateral Forum for Dialogue did not exist any longer and should be replaced with a new mechanism for local cooperation in which the people of the Campo de Gibraltar and Gibraltar were represented;

(d) Welcomed the efforts made by all to resolve problems and advance in a spirit of trust and solidarity, in order to find common solutions and move forward in areas of mutual interest towards a relationship based on dialogue and cooperation.

75/524. Proposed programme of work and timetable of the Special Political and Decolonization Committee (Fourth Committee) for the seventy-sixth session of the General Assembly

At its 41st plenary meeting, on 10 December 2020, the General Assembly, on the recommendation of the Special Political and Decolonization Committee (Fourth Committee),[66] approved the proposed programme of work and timetable of the Fourth Committee for the seventy-sixth session of the Assembly, as set out in the report of the Committee.[67]

75/525. Programme planning (Special Political and Decolonization Committee (Fourth Committee))

At its 41st plenary meeting, on 10 December 2020, the General Assembly took note of the report of the Special Political and Decolonization Committee (Fourth Committee).[68]

4. *Decisions adopted on the reports of the Second Committee*

75/543. Macroeconomic policy questions

At its 48th plenary meeting, on 21 December 2020, the General Assembly took note of the report of the Second Committee.[69]

75/544. Globalization and interdependence

At its 48th plenary meeting, on 21 December 2020, the General Assembly took note of the report of the Second Committee.[70]

---

[65] A/75/420, para. 28.

[66] A/75/422, para. 6.

[67] A/75/422.

[68] A/75/421.

[69] A/75/455.

[70] A/75/460.

75/545. Groups of countries in special situations

At its 48th plenary meeting, on 21 December 2020, the General Assembly took note of the report of the Second Committee.[71]

75/546. Operational activities for development

At its 48th plenary meeting, on 21 December 2020, the General Assembly took note of the report of the Second Committee.[72]

75/547. Draft programme of work of the Second Committee for the seventy-sixth session of the General Assembly

At its 48th plenary meeting, on 21 December 2020, the General Assembly, on the recommendation of the Second Committee:[73]

(a) Approved, subject to any subsequent decision by the Assembly, the draft programme of work of the Second Committee for the seventy-sixth session of the Assembly as set out below;

(b) Invited the Bureau of the Second Committee at the seventy-sixth session, in preparing the draft programme of work and timetable of the Committee for the seventy-sixth session, to take into account the provisional programme of work and timetable of the Committee as contained in document A/C.2/75/CRP.3.

Draft programme of work[74]

1.   Information and communications technologies for sustainable development.

2.   Macroeconomic policy questions:

    (a)   International trade and development;

    (b)   International financial system and development;

    (c)   External debt sustainability and development;

    (d)   Commodities;

    (e)   Financial inclusion for sustainable development;

    (f)   Promotion of international cooperation to combat illicit financial flows and strengthen good practices on assets return to foster sustainable development;

    (g)   Promoting investments for sustainable development.

3.   Follow-up to and implementation of the outcomes of the International Conferences on Financing for Development.

4.   Sustainable development:

    (a)   Towards the achievement of sustainable development: implementation of the 2030 Agenda for Sustainable Development, including through sustainable consumption and production, building on Agenda 21;

---

[71] A/75/461.

[72] A/75/463.

[73] A/75/467, para. 9.

[74] The final list of items and sub-items to be considered will be based on the resolutions and decisions adopted by the General Assembly.

    (b)   Follow-up to and implementation of the SIDS Accelerated Modalities of Action (SAMOA) Pathway and the Mauritius Strategy for the Further Implementation of the Programme of Action for the Sustainable Development of Small Island Developing States;

    (c)   Disaster risk reduction;

    (d)   Protection of global climate for present and future generations of humankind;

    (e)   Implementation of the United Nations Convention to Combat Desertification in Those Countries Experiencing Serious Drought and/or Desertification, Particularly in Africa;

    (f)   Convention on Biological Diversity;

    (g)   Report of the United Nations Environment Assembly of the United Nations Environment Programme;

    (h)   Education for sustainable development;

    (i)   Ensuring access to affordable, reliable, sustainable and modern energy for all;

    (j)   Combating sand and dust storms;

    (k)   Strengthening cooperation for integrated coastal zone management for achieving sustainable development.

5.   Globalization and interdependence:

    (a)   Science, technology and innovation for sustainable development;

    (b)   Culture and sustainable development;

    (c)   Development cooperation with middle-income countries.

6.   Groups of countries in special situations:

    (a)   Follow-up to the Fourth United Nations Conference on the Least Developed Countries;

    (b)   Follow-up to the second United Nations Conference on Landlocked Developing Countries.

7.   Eradication of poverty and other development issues:

    (a)   Implementation of the Third United Nations Decade for the Eradication of Poverty (2018–2027);

    (b)   Eradicating rural poverty to implement the 2030 Agenda for Sustainable Development.

8.   Operational activities for development:

    (a)   Operational activities for development of the United Nations system;

    (b)   South-South cooperation for development.

9.   Agriculture development, food security and nutrition:

    (a)   Agriculture development, food security and nutrition;

    (b)   Natural plant fibres and sustainable development.

10.   Towards global partnerships.

11.   Permanent sovereignty of the Palestinian people in the Occupied Palestinian Territory, including East Jerusalem, and of the Arab population in the occupied Syrian Golan over their natural resources.

75/548. Revitalization of the work of the Second Committee

At its 48th plenary meeting, on 21 December 2020, the General Assembly, on the recommendation of the Second Committee:[75]

(a)   Recalled its resolutions 73/341 of 12 September 2019 and 74/303 of 4 September 2020 and its decision 74/537 B of 11 August 2020;

(b)   Decided that the Bureau of the Second Committee would convene informal dialogues to discuss the revitalization of the work of the Committee in the first months of 2021;

(c)   Also decided that the Second Committee would convene a plenary meeting following those dialogues to take stock of the deliberations and, as appropriate, take action on any recommendations, for subsequent approval by the General Assembly, to allow any change to come into effect ahead of the seventy-sixth session.

75/549. Programme planning (Second Committee)

At its 48th plenary meeting, on 21 December 2020, the General Assembly took note of the report of the Second Committee.[76]

5. *Decisions adopted on the reports of the Third Committee*

75/537. Promotion and protection of human rights

At its 46th plenary meeting, on 16 December 2020, the General Assembly took note of the report of the Third Committee.[77]

75/538. Comprehensive implementation of and follow-up to the Vienna Declaration and Programme of Action

At its 46th plenary meeting, on 16 December 2020, the General Assembly took note of the report of the Third Committee.[78]

75/539. Countering the use of information and communications technologies for criminal purposes

At its 46th plenary meeting, on 16 December 2020, the General Assembly took note of the report of the Third Committee.[79]

75/540. Draft programme of work of the Third Committee for the seventy-sixth session of the General Assembly

At its 46th meeting, on 16 December 2020, the General Assembly, on the recommendation of the Third Committee:[80]

(a)   Approved, subject to any subsequent decision by the Assembly, the draft programme of work of the Third Committee for the seventy-sixth session of the Assembly as set out below;

---

[75] A/75/467, para. 9.

[76] A/75/466.

[77] A/75/478.

[78] A/75/478/Add.4.

[79] A/75/480.

[80] A/75/482, para. 7.

(b)   Invited the Bureau of the Third Committee at the seventy-sixth session, in preparing the draft programme of work and timetable of the Committee for the seventy-sixth session, to take into account the draft provisional programme of work and timetable of the Committee as contained in document A/C.3/75/CRP.1.

Draft programme of work

Item 1.   Social development:

(a)   Implementation of the outcome of the World Summit for Social Development and of the twenty-fourth special session of the General Assembly;

(b)   Social development, including questions relating to the world social situation and to youth, ageing, persons with disabilities and the family.

Item 2.   Crime prevention and criminal justice.

Item 3.   International drug control.

Item 4.   Advancement of women:

(a)   Advancement of women;

(b)   Implementation of the outcome of the Fourth World Conference on Women and of the twenty-third special session of the General Assembly.

Item 5.   Promotion and protection of the rights of children:

(a)   Promotion and protection of the rights of children;

(b)   Follow-up to the outcome of the special session on children.

Item 6.   Rights of indigenous peoples:

(a)   Rights of indigenous peoples;

(b)   Follow-up to the outcome document of the high-level plenary meeting of the General Assembly known as the World Conference on Indigenous Peoples.

Item 7.   Promotion and protection of human rights:

(a)   Implementation of human rights instruments;

(b)   Human rights questions, including alternative approaches for improving the effective enjoyment of human rights and fundamental freedoms;

(c)   Human rights situations and reports of special rapporteurs and representatives;

(d)   Comprehensive implementation of and follow-up to the Vienna Declaration and Programme of Action.

Item 8.   Elimination of racism, racial discrimination, xenophobia and related intolerance:

(a)   Elimination of racism, racial discrimination, xenophobia and related intolerance;

(b)   Comprehensive implementation of and follow-up to the Durban Declaration and Programme of Action.

Item 9.   Right of peoples to self-determination.

Item 10.   Report of the Human Rights Council.

Item 11.   Report of the United Nations High Commissioner for Refugees, questions relating to refugees, returnees and displaced persons and humanitarian questions.

Item 12.   Revitalization of the work of the General Assembly.

75/541. Programme planning (Third Committee)

At its 46th plenary meeting, on 16 December 2020, the General Assembly took note of the report of the Third Committee.[81]

6. *Decisions adopted on the reports of the Fifth Committee*

75/553. Questions deferred for future consideration

At its 48th (resumed) plenary meeting, on 31 December 2020, the General Assembly, on the recommendation of the Fifth Committee,[82]

Section A

Decided to defer until the first part of its resumed seventy-fifth session consideration of the following documents:

Item 141
Programme budget for 2021

Review of the experience of the utilization of the contingency fund

Report of the Secretary-General on the review of the experience of the utilization of the contingency fund[83]

Related report of the Advisory Committee on Administrative and Budgetary Questions[84]

Section B

Decided to defer until the main part of its seventy-sixth session consideration of the following documents:

Item 139
Review of the efficiency of the administrative and financial functioning of the United Nations

Shifting the management paradigm in the United Nations: budgetary procedures and practices

Report of the Secretary-General entitled "Shifting the management paradigm in the United Nations: budgetary procedures and practices"[85]

Related report of the Advisory Committee on Administrative and Budgetary Questions[86]

Item 141
Programme budget for 2021

Estimates in respect of special political missions, good offices and other political initiatives authorized by the General Assembly and/or the Security Council

Report of the Secretary-General on the review of arrangements for funding and backstopping special political missions[87]

Related report of the Advisory Committee on Administrative and Budgetary Questions[88]

---

[81] A/75/483.

[82] A/75/683, para. 6.

[83] A/70/395.

[84] A/70/7/Add.7.

[85] A/74/852.

[86] A/74/7/Add.33.

[87] A/66/340.

[88] A/66/7/Add.21.

7. *Decisions adopted on the reports of the Sixth Committee*

75/526. Protection of persons in the event of disasters

At its 45th plenary meeting, on 15 December 2020, the General Assembly, on the recommendation of the Sixth Committee,[89] decided to defer the consideration of the item entitled "Protection of persons in the event of disasters" to the seventy-sixth session of the Assembly.

75/527. Provisional programme of work of the Sixth Committee for the seventy-sixth session of the General Assembly

At its 45th plenary meeting, on 15 December 2020, the General Assembly, on the recommendation of the Sixth Committee,[90] noted that the Committee had decided to adopt the following provisional programme of work for the seventy-sixth session of the Assembly, as proposed by the Bureau:

Provisional programme of work[91]

4 October	Organization of work of the Sixth Committee
4 to 6 October	Measures to eliminate international terrorism
6 and 7 October	Criminal accountability of United Nations officials and experts on mission
7 and 8 October	The rule of law at the national and international levels
8 October	Crimes against humanity
11 October	Administration of justice at the United Nations
11 and 12 October	Strengthening and promoting the international treaty framework
12 and 13 October	The scope and application of the principle of universal jurisdiction
15 October	Report of the Special Committee on the Charter of the United Nations and on the Strengthening of the Role of the Organization
	Protection of persons in the event of disasters
18 October	Report of the United Nations Commission on International Trade Law on the work of its fifty-fourth session
19 October	Request(s) for observer status
21 October	Report of the Committee on Relations with the Host Country
22 October	United Nations Programme of Assistance in the Teaching, Study, Dissemination and Wider Appreciation of International Law

---

[89] A/75/435, para. 7.

[90] A/75/453 and A/74/453/Corr.1, para. 6.

[91] Indicating provisional dates in 2021 for debates under the respective items without prejudice to the allocation of additional meetings for working groups established and Secretariat briefings convened by the Sixth Committee.

25 to 29 October and 2 and 3 November	Report of the International Law Commission on the work of its seventy-second session
8 November	Revitalization of the work of the General Assembly
18 November	Programme planning
	Election of the officers of the Main Committees
14 and 22 October and 17 November	Reserved

75/528. Programme planning (Sixth Committee)

At its 45th plenary meeting, on 15 December 2020, the General Assembly took note of the report of the Sixth Committee.[92]

75/529. Observer status for the Cooperation Council of Turkic-speaking States in the General Assembly

At its 45th plenary meeting, on 15 December 2020, the General Assembly, on the recommendation of the Sixth Committee,[93] decided to defer a decision on the request for observer status for the Cooperation Council of Turkic-speaking States in the Assembly[94] until the seventy-sixth session of the Assembly.

75/530. Observer status for the Eurasian Economic Union in the General Assembly

At its 45th plenary meeting, on 15 December 2020, the General Assembly, on the recommendation of the Sixth Committee,[95] decided to defer a decision on the request for observer status for the Eurasian Economic Union in the Assembly[96] until the seventy-sixth session of the Assembly.

75/531. Observer status for the Community of Democracies in the General Assembly

At its 45th plenary meeting, on 15 December 2020, the General Assembly, on the recommendation of the Sixth Committee,[97] decided to defer a decision on the request for observer status for the Community of Democracies in the Assembly[98] until the seventy-sixth session of the Assembly.

75/532. Observer status for the Ramsar Convention on Wetlands Secretariat in the General Assembly

At its 45th plenary meeting, on 15 December 2020, the General Assembly, on the recommendation of the Sixth Committee,[99] decided to defer a decision on the request for observer status for the Ramsar Convention on Wetlands Secretariat in the Assembly[100] until the seventy-sixth session of the Assembly.

---

[92] A/75/452.

[93] A/75/440, para. 7.

[94] See A/66/141.

[95] A/75/441, para. 7.

[96] See A/70/141.

[97] A/75/442, para. 7.

[98] See A/70/142.

[99] A/75/443, para. 7.

[100] See A/72/194.

75/533. Observer status for the Global Environment Facility in the General Assembly

At its 45th plenary meeting, on 15 December 2020, the General Assembly, on the recommendation of the Sixth Committee,[101] decided to defer a decision on the request for observer status for the Global Environment Facility in the Assembly[102] until the seventy-sixth session of the Assembly.

75/534. Observer status for the International Organization of Employers in the General Assembly

At its 45th plenary meeting, on 15 December 2020, the General Assembly, on the recommendation of the Sixth Committee,[103] decided to defer a decision on the request for observer status for the International Organization of Employers in the Assembly[104] until the seventy-sixth session of the Assembly.

75/535. Observer status for the International Trade Union Confederation in the General Assembly

At its 45th plenary meeting, on 15 December 2020, the General Assembly, on the recommendation of the Sixth Committee,[105] decided to defer a decision on the request for observer status for the International Trade Union Confederation in the Assembly[106] until the seventy-sixth session of the Assembly.

75/536. Observer status for the Boao Forum for Asia in the General Assembly

At its 45th plenary meeting, on 15 December 2020, the General Assembly, on the recommendation of the Sixth Committee,[107] decided to defer a decision on the request for observer status for the Boao Forum for Asia in the Assembly[108] until the seventy-sixth session of the Assembly.

---

[101] A/75/444, para. 7.

[102] See A/72/195.

[103] A/75/445, para. 7.

[104] See A/74/291.

[105] A/75/446, para. 7.

[106] See A/74/292.

[107] A/75/447, para. 7.

[108] See A/74/293.

Annex

Checklist of decisions

Decision number	Title	Item	Plenary meeting	Date of adoption	Page
75/401.	Appointment of the members of the Credentials Committee	3 (a)	1st	15 September 2020	4
75/402.	Election of members of the Human Rights Council	119 (c)	16th	13 October 2020	4
75/403.	Election of members of the International Court of Justice	118 (c)	24th	12 November 2020	4
75/404.	Appointment of members of the Advisory Committee on Administrative and Budgetary Questions	120 (a)	30th	23 November 2020	5
75/405.	Appointment of members of the Committee on Contributions	120 (b)	30th	23 November 2020	5
75/406.	Confirmation of the appointment of members of the Investments Committee	120 (c)	30th	23 November 2020	6
75/407.	Appointment of members of the International Civil Service Commission	120 (d)	30th	23 November 2020	6
75/408.	Appointment of members of the Independent Audit Advisory Committee	120 (e)	30th 48th (resumed)	23 November 2020 31 December 2020	7
75/409.	Appointment of members and alternate members of the United Nations Staff Pension Committee	120 (f)	30th	23 November 2020	7
75/410.	Election of members of the Committee for Programme and Coordination	119 (a)	30th 48th	23 November 2020 21 December 2020	7
75/411.	Election of the United Nations High Commissioner for Refugees	119 (d)	30th	23 November 2020	8
75/412.	Appointment of members of the Committee on Conferences	120 (g)	30th	23 November 2020	8
75/413.	Election of members of the Organizational Committee of the Peacebuilding Commission	119 (b)	44th	14 December 2020	8
75/501.	Organization of the seventy-fifth session	7	2nd 30th 35th 46th	18 September 2020 23 November 2020 2 December 2020 16 December 2020	10
75/502.	General debate of the seventy-fifth session of the General Assembly	7	2nd	18 September 2020	10
75/503.	High-level meeting to commemorate the seventy-fifth anniversary of the United Nations	7	2nd	18 September 2020	10
75/504.	Adoption of the agenda and allocation of agenda items	7	2nd 30th	18 September 2020 23 November 2020	11
75/505.	High-level meeting of the General Assembly to commemorate the seventy-fifth anniversary of the United Nations	128 (a)	15th	29 September 2020	11

Decision number	Title	Item	Plenary meeting	Date of adoption	Page
75/506.	Introduction of certain reports in the plenary meetings at the seventy-fifth session of the General Assembly	7	16th	13 October 2020	12
75/507.	Report of the International Residual Mechanism for Criminal Tribunals	132	17th	21 October 2020	12
75/508.	Report of the International Court of Justice	74	20th	3 November 2020	12
75/509.	Report of the Economic and Social Council	9	21st	5 November 2020	12
75/510.	Procedure for decision-making in the General Assembly when an in-person meeting is not possible	126	26th	13 November 2020	12
75/511.	United Nations Pledging Conference for Development Activities	7 and 25	30th	23 November 2020	14
75/512.	Reduction of military budgets	94	37th	7 December 2020	20
75/513.	Maintenance of international security – good-neighbourliness, stability and development in South-Eastern Europe	97	37th	7 December 2020	21
75/514.	Further practical measures for the prevention of an arms race in outer space	101 (c)	37th	7 December 2020	21
75/515.	Treaty banning the production of fissile material for nuclear weapons or other nuclear explosive devices	103 (a)	37th	7 December 2020	21
75/516.	Nuclear disarmament verification	103 (mm)	37th	7 December 2020	21
75/517.	Compliance with non-proliferation, arms limitation and disarmament agreements and commitments	103 (ff)	37th	7 December 2020	21
75/518.	Missiles	103 (s)	37th	7 December 2020	22
75/519.	Disarmament Commission	105 (b)	37th	7 December 2020	22
75/520.	Provisional programme of work and timetable of the First Committee for 2021	126	37th	7 December 2020	22
75/521.	Programme planning (First Committee)	142	37th	7 December 2020	22
75/522.	Comprehensive review of the whole question of peacekeeping operations in all their aspects	54	41st	10 December 2020	23
75/523.	Question of Gibraltar	61	41st	10 December 2020	24
75/524.	Proposed programme of work and timetable of the Special Political and Decolonization Committee (Fourth Committee) for the seventy-sixth session of the General Assembly	126	41st	10 December 2020	24
75/525.	Programme planning (Special Political and Decolonization Committee (Fourth Committee))	142	41st	10 December 2020	24
75/526.	Protection of persons in the event of disasters	89	45th	15 December 2020	30
75/527.	Provisional programme of work of the Sixth Committee for the seventy-sixth session of the General Assembly	126	45th	15 December 2020	30
75/528.	Programme planning (Sixth Committee)	142	45th	15 December 2020	31

Decision number	Title	Item	Plenary meeting	Date of adoption	Page
75/529.	Observer status for the Cooperation Council of Turkic-speaking States in the General Assembly	172	45th	15 December 2020	31
75/530.	Observer status for the Eurasian Economic Union in the General Assembly	173	45th	15 December 2020	31
75/531.	Observer status for the Community of Democracies in the General Assembly	174	45th	15 December 2020	31
75/532.	Observer status for the Ramsar Convention on Wetlands Secretariat in the General Assembly	175	45th	15 December 2020	31
75/533.	Observer status for the Global Environment Facility in the General Assembly	176	45th	15 December 2020	32
75/534.	Observer status for the International Organization of Employers in the General Assembly	177	45th	15 December 2020	32
75/535.	Observer status for the International Trade Union Confederation in the General Assembly	178	45th	15 December 2020	32
75/536.	Observer status for the Boao Forum for Asia in the General Assembly	179	45th	15 December 2020	32
75/537.	Promotion and protection of human rights	72	46th	16 December 2020	27
75/538.	Comprehensive implementation of and follow-up to the Vienna Declaration and Programme of Action	72 (d)	46th	16 December 2020	27
75/539.	Countering the use of information and communications technologies for criminal purposes	112	46th	16 December 2020	27
75/540.	Draft programme of work of the Third Committee for the seventy-sixth session of the General Assembly	126	46th	16 December 2020	27
75/541.	Programme planning (Third Committee)	142	46th	16 December 2020	29
75/542.	Investigation into the conditions and circumstances resulting in the tragic death of Dag Hammarskjöld and of the members of the party accompanying him	133	47th	21 December 2020	15
75/543.	Macroeconomic policy questions	17	48th	21 December 2020	24
75/544.	Globalization and interdependence	22	48th	21 December 2020	24
75/545.	Groups of countries in special situations	23	48th	21 December 2020	25
75/546.	Operational activities for development	25	48th	21 December 2020	25
75/547.	Draft programme of work of the Second Committee for the seventy-sixth session of the General Assembly	126	48th	21 December 2020	25
75/548.	Revitalization of the work of the Second Committee	126	48th	21 December 2020	27
75/549.	Programme planning (Second Committee)	142	48th	21 December 2020	27

Decision number	Title	Item	Plenary meeting	Date of adoption	Page
75/550.	Open-ended Working Group on Developments in the Field of Information and Telecommunications in the Context of International Security established pursuant to General Assembly resolution 73/27 of 5 December 2018	98	48th (resumed)	31 December 2020	22
75/551.	Group of Governmental Experts on Advancing Responsible State Behaviour in Cyberspace in the Context of International Security established pursuant to General Assembly resolution 73/266 of 22 December 2018	98	48th (resumed)	31 December 2020	23
75/552.	Problems arising from the accumulation of conventional ammunition stockpiles in surplus	103 (z)	48th (resumed)	31 December 2020	23
75/553.	Questions deferred for future consideration	139	48th (resumed)	31 December 2020	29
75/554.	Agenda items remaining for consideration by the General Assembly at its seventy-fifth session	7	48th (resumed)	31 December 2020	15